Ceramic Painting
made easy

Series Editors: Susan & Martin Penny

David & Charles

A DAVID & CHARLES BOOK

First published in the UK in 1999

A catalogue record for this book is available from the British Library.

ISBN 0 7153 0891 2

Series Editors: Susan & Martin Penny
Designed and produced by Penny & Penny
Illustrations: Fred Fieber at Red Crayola
Photography: Jon Stone

Printed in Italy by LEGO SpA, Vicenza
for David & Charles
Brunel House Newton Abbot Devon

Contents

	Introduction	6
	Transferring the Design	8
	Painting Techniques	9
	Hints and Tips	13
Project	Floral Kitchen Set	14
Project	Painted Flower Pots	18
Project	Art Deco Cruet Set	24
Project	Maritime Tiles	28
Project	Freehand Painted Mugs	34
Project	Finger Painted Teapots	38
Project	French Tiles	40
Project	Malachite Coffee Set	50
Project	Mediterranean Bowls	54
Project	Animal Breakfast Set	58
	Acknowledgements	62
	Suppliers	63
	Index	64

Introduction to Ceramic Painting

Ceramic Painting Made Easy is a complete guide to the craft of ceramic painting; read on for useful advice on choosing the correct china; understanding paint and its uses; help with choosing the correct brush; trying out new decorative finishes; and all the advice and guidance you need to help you paint ceramics at home, without a kiln

Essential equipment

Below is a list of equipment needed when ceramic painting:

- **Brushes** – use only natural hair brushes, to reduce lines and produce a smoother effect.
- **Paper** – use copier paper to make a tracing of the design.
- **Typewriter carbon paper** – used for transferring a design to the china.
- **Alcohol** – used for wiping the surface of the china before painting to remove greasy marks, and to help the paint to adhere to the surface of the china.
- **Chinagraph pencil** – for marking design lines on to the china.
- **Stencil brush** – used with a stencil for applying paint to china.
- **Paint dish** – flat plastic microwave dish or fresh food tray.
- **Kitchen paper** – for mopping up spills.
- **Cotton buds** – used for correcting mistakes.
- **Soft sponge** – used to 'sponge' paint on to the surface of the glass.
- **Plastic bag** – used to create a 'bagging' effect on the china.
- **Masking tape** – used to mask off areas of china that you do not want to paint, and as guides for painting straight lines.
- **Hair dryer** – useful for drying paint between colour changes.
- **Cutting knife** – used for 'scratching' a design in the dry paint.
- **Oven** – used for hardening the paint.

Which brush ?

- ✔ Use a decorator's brush to create a 'dragged' effect with the paint
- ✔ Paint hazy landscapes and greenery with a fan-shaped brush

- ✔ Use a comb brush for filling in the background areas
- ✔ A brush called dagger stripper should be used for flower and leaf shapes
- ✔ Use a round brush for filling in
- ✔ Lines and outlines should be drawn with a fine liner brush
- ✔ For covering large areas quickly use a sponge brush
- ✔ Use a stencil brush for 'pouncing' paint through a stencil

Tips for painting on china

- ✔ China must be squeaky clean before painting
- ✔ Lay the china on a pad of kitchen paper
- ✔ Apply even coats of paint
- ✔ Do not rush the painting; allow plenty of drying time between colours
- ✔ Clean equipment and brushes regularly

Selecting china

- Any non-porous, kiln hardened, white or coloured china can be used for painting.
- Porous surfaces like flower pots should be sealed with filler undercoat before painting.

Selecting paint

Porcelain paint can be used on all types of china, and once oven hardened will stand up to normal use in the kitchen.

Ceramic paint is a solvent based, cold-set paint: this means it will harden without being heated. The paint is not heat resistant, so use for decorative purposes only, and where it will not come in contact with food. Some ceramic paint may need to be varnished.

Decorative effects

- ✔ Use a decorator's brush to 'drag' paint
- ✔ Use scrunched plastic for 'bagging'
- ✔ Cut-up a household sponge for 'sponging'
- ✔ Use your finger to 'dot and dab' paint
- ✔ Create a marbled effect with a fan paintbrush
- ✔ Decorate china using a stencil

Hardening oven dry paint

- ✔ Check the paint instructions to see if it needs to be oven hardened
- ✔ Allow painted china to air dry for between 24 hours and 7 days before baking
- ✔ Place the dry painted china in a cold oven, and set the oven temperature to gas mark 2/3, 300/325°F (150/170°C)
- ✔ Bake for 30-35 minutes, timing from when the oven temperature stabilizes
- ✔ Do not remove the baked china from the oven until it has cooled
- ✔ There may be a slight odour during baking, but this is non-toxic and harmless

Choosing the right paint

To help you understand a little more about the paint you will be working with, listed below are some of the plus and minus points for each paint.

- **Porcelain paint** – Water-based
  The most durable paint for ceramics
  Drying time 24 hours – 7 days
  Needs to be thermohardened in an oven
  Baking time 35 minutes
  Gas mark 2/3, 300/325°F (150/170°C)
  Will stand normal use in the kitchen
  Not dishwasher safe
- **Ceramic paint** – Solvent-based (cold set)
  Sets in about two days, without baking
  Use for decorative purposes only
  Brushes can be washed in water
  Paint must be cleaned from brushes using white spirit, or a cleaner recommended by the paint manufacturer; brushes should then be washed in water, before drying thoroughly
- **Porcelain outliner paste**
  Easy to use, squeeze like an icing tube
  Needs to be thermohardened in an oven
- **Gloss medium**
  Mix with paint to produce a lighter tone
  Will not thin paint
  Blend 1/3 medium to 2/3 paint
- **Matt medium**
  Gives paint a matt effect
  Use as an undercoat or mix with paint

- **Filler undercoat**
  Seals porous surfaces like flower pots
  Use as an undercoat

Transferring the Design

Most designs are best transferred on to the surface of the china with a tracing and typewriter carbon paper; some less complex designs can be painted through a stencil; and straight lines can be drawn before painting using a chinagraph pencil, or by painting between masking tape grids

Using carbon paper

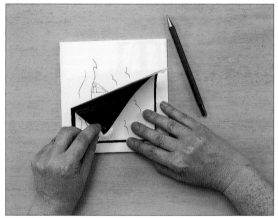

To transfer the design, place typewriter carbon paper between the china and the tracing. Draw over the design lines with a ball-point. Carefully remove the tracing and carbon.

Using a stencil

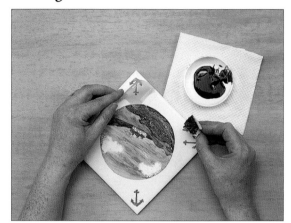

Cut the design from stencil film or acetate, using a sharp craft knife. Attach the stencil to the china using masking tape, then sponge or paint on to the cut out shape.

Using paper masks

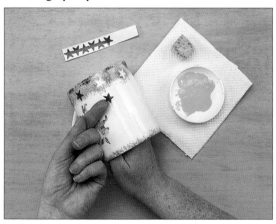

Create interesting border designs using self-adhesive shapes (bought from stationers): attach the shapes to the china, then sponge or paint over the top; when dry peel off.

Using masking tape grids

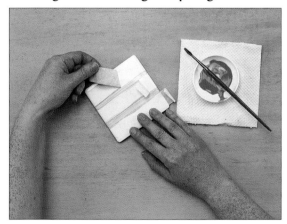

To help when painting straight lines on china, attach two rows of masking tape firmly to the china and then paint between the tape. When the paint is dry remove the tape.

Painting Techniques

Although ceramic painting may look difficult, no special skills are needed to produce spectacular results. Use air dry ceramic paint on china that will be used for display; for a more durable finish use oven hardened porcelain paint. Check the suggested usage on the manufacturer's instructions before starting

Brushes and brush strokes

Use a decorator's brush for dragging; fan or sponge brush for landscapes; comb for backgrounds; dagger stripper for flowers; round brush for filling in, and a liner for lines.

Using gloss medium

Use gloss medium to produce a lighter tone of the same colour, without thinning the consistency of the paint: blend approximately $1/3$ medium to $2/3$ paint.

Building up coats of paint

Porcelain and ceramic paint comes in semi-transparent, transparent and opaque colours. Build up the coats, allowing drying time between each application.

Mixing paint

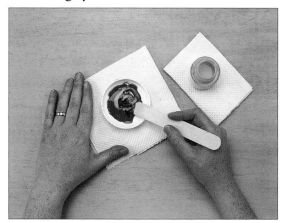

To blend colour: pour a small amount of the darker coloured paint into a dish and then slowly add the lighter, blending until the paint is thoroughly mixed together.

Freehand brush strokes

Lines can be painted freehand or add chinagraph pencil lines as a guide. Dip a fine liner brush into paint: do not overload or the paint will blob. Holding the china firmly with one hand, pull the brush steadily across the china. Always paint towards you, turning the china as you go.

Adding outlines

Outlines can be added to the design in several different ways: using outliner paste which comes in a tube, and should be squeezed like an icing bag; by decanting porcelain paint into a dropper bottle then attaching a fine nib; or painting around the outlines with a fine brush.

Using matt medium

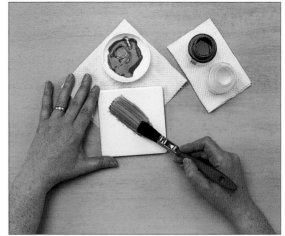

To give paint a matt effect when baked: apply a coat of matt medium to the china, before painting. When dry, paint with porcelain paint. Matt medium can also be mixed with the paint: apply several even coats to the china, or the paint may become streaky when hardened.

Scratching off

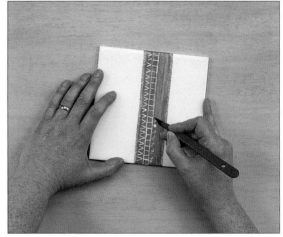

Use a template and carbon paper to transfer the design lines on to the dry but unhardened painted china; using the point of a sharp knife, scratch away the design lines. Alternatively, scratch the design freehand. Scratching can be used for intricate patterns: rather than painting them on, you can scratch them off.

Sponging on

Mask off any areas that you do not want to be painted with masking tape. Load a small piece of washing-up sponge with paint, then pounce it on and off the china creating a mottled effect. Continue to load the sponge with paint and pounce until the china is covered. When dry remove the tape.

Dragging

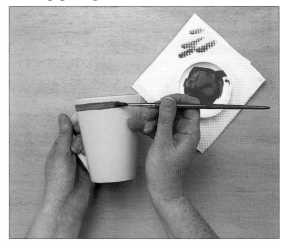

Keeping even pressure on the brush, drag it over the china in a smooth even movement: this will leave a dragged line on the china. Take care not to smudge the paint if you are painting a circular object like a mug or bowl. To help paint straight, add simple guide lines with a chinagraph.

Bagging

Apply a coat of paint to the china, then take a very small piece of plastic bag and scrunch it into a ball. While the paint is still wet, use the scrunched plastic to lift off the paint in a quick pouncing motion. Renew the scrunched plastic at regular intervals to avoid a build-up of paint.

Finger painting

Cut a piece of towelling large enough to wrap around your index finger. Dip your finger into the paint, then dab and dot it on to the china in groups of two, three or four. Build up the colours in this way, using a fresh piece of towelling for each. Continue the process for a deeper finish.

Marbling

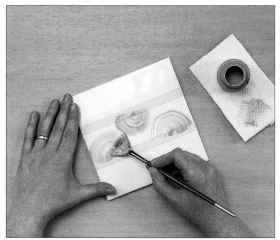

Using a fan paintbrush, apply swirls to the china in a tight circular movement. Keep the brush almost vertical, and the bristles in contact with the china to provide a continuous flow of paint; make crimps in some of the swirls to give a ripple effect. The first row should be on alternate sides, just touching, but not overlapping.

Before the paint dries, make more swirls in two different colours, in the gaps between, and overlapping the first swirls. Use gold paint very lightly over the top of the swirls, using the same brush movement as for the other colours: in some areas the gold paint should hardly be visible.

Using filler undercoat

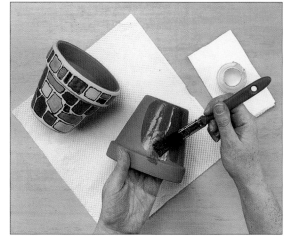

If you are painting on a porous surface, first paint over it with a coat of filler undercoat: this will act as a primer and prevents the china soaking up the paint. Allow at least 2 hours drying time before painting. The china will need to air dry for 7 days before hardening, because of the number of coats.

Washing brushes

For the best results, invest in natural hair brushes for ceramic painting. To prolong their life: wash them regularly in warm water while in use – this will stop a build-up of paint and keep them in good condition. If you are using solvent-based paint, clean the brushes in white spirit before washing.

Hints and Tips

Making sure that the china is squeaky clean will ensure that the paint adheres properly to the surface: clean in warm soapy water before wiping again with alcohol to remove any greasy marks. Depending on the numbers of coats used, allow between 24 hours and 7 days to dry before oven hardening

Cleaning with alcohol

Before painting, clean the china in warm soapy water. When dry, wipe with alcohol to remove any oily deposits: this will enable the paint to adhere to the surface of the china.

Quick drying

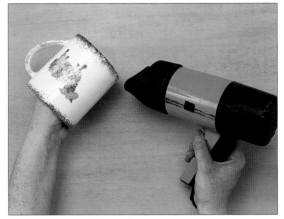

If you are working on a very complex design and need to dry the paint between colour changes: use a hair dryer on the lowest heat setting to touch dry the paint.

Correcting mistakes

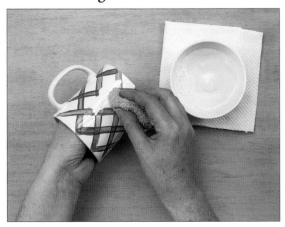

Mistakes can easily be wiped away using moist kitchen paper or a cotton bud. If the piece has been left to dry, scrubbing with warm water may be necessary.

Oven baking

If you are using paint that has to be oven baked, place the china in a cold oven. Set to gas mark 2/3, 300/325°F (150/170°C).When the oven stabilizes, bake for 30-35 minutes.

Floral Kitchen Set

Bring summer into your kitchen all year round with this pretty hand-painted kitchen set. The butter dish and storage jar have been painted with daisies, in bright shades of yellow, pink and blue; whereas the jug is painted with a single sunflower and the background sponged in turquoise

You will need

- White china butter dish, pot and jug
- Water-based porcelain paint – deep yellow, bright yellow, royal blue, ming blue, fuschia, deep lilac, orange, amber, turquoise, sage green, brown
- Porcelain outliner – gold
- Small paintbrushes
- White paper, pencil
- Chinagraph pencil, scissors
- Container of water, kitchen paper, masking tape
- Alcohol, small piece of sponge

Preparing the china

1 Wash the china in warm soapy water and dry thoroughly.

2 Using kitchen paper, wipe the surface of the china with alcohol, then leave to dry: the alcohol will remove any greasy marks and help the paint adhere to the surface of the china.

Transferring the design

1 Lay white paper over the flower motifs on page 17. Trace over the designs carefully using a soft pencil. You can use a photocopier if you would prefer not to mark your book or if you need to enlarge or reduce the size of the design to fit your china.

Painting the butter dish

1 Cut the centre ring from the daisy tracing. Position the tracing on the china, drawing around the inner and outer edges of the ring. Re-position the tracing and repeat as many times as you need to cover the butter dish and pot, remembering to allow enough room around each flower for the petal tips.

2 Working on one flower at a time, paint each petal with single brush stroke using a fine paintbrush, radiating out from the inner circle to just over the outer circle; leave gaps between the petals for the lighter petals. Paint the daisies in royal blue, deep yellow and

fuchsia mixed with deep lilac paint. Wash the brush in clean water and dry on kitchen paper between each colour. Leave the paint to dry for at least 30 minutes.

3 Complete the daisies by adding more petals into the gaps, using ming blue, bright yellow and fuchsia paint, leave to dry.

4 Paint the centre of each flower orange; when dry overpaint with a ring of amber just on the outer half of the orange circle. Using a fine paintbrush and amber paint, add detail lines to separate the petals on the yellow flowers. Dot gold outliner on to the centre of each flower.

5 To fill the background area of the design: dip a piece of kitchen sponge into turquoise paint and carefully pounce the sponge on to the china, using a circular movement. Work on one small area at a time, taking care not to sponge over the petals. Do not apply too much paint to the sponge or it will leave a heavy impression the china. Repeat with the sage green paint, then leave to dry for 48 hours.

Painting the sunflower jug

1 Cover the handle and the top edge of the jug 2.5cm (1in) below the rim with masking tape, snipping the tape if necessary to make it lay flat.

2 Cut out the sunflower tracing around the outer edge of the petals, and around the inner circle. Attach the sunflower tracing centrally on one side of the jug, using double sided tape. Draw around the petals and inner circle with a chinagraph pencil.

3 Paint the petals in bright yellow, using a medium paintbrush; add highlight in deep yellow and amber.

4 Paint a circle in the centre of the sunflower using brown, then, when dry, overpaint the outer half of the circle with amber paint. Leave the paint to dry, then apply orange dots to the sunflower centre.

5 Using the same method as before, pounce turquoise and sage green paint on to the background of the jug, using a piece of sponge (see Painting Techniques, page 11). Leave a

circular unpainted border around the sunflower. Allow to dry for 48 hours.

6 Carefully remove the masking tape and then paint a bright yellow zig-zag line on the rim of the jug and on the handle. Fill in the triangular area below each zig-zag with turquoise paint.

Drying time

1 Allow the paint to air dry for a full 48 hours before hardening: if the paint has been applied thickly allow a longer drying time. Bubbling may occur during hardening if the paint is not completely dry.

Hardening the paint

1 It is necessary to thermoharden water-based porcelain paint in a domestic oven to make it strong enough to stand up to normal use in the kitchen, although it would be advisable not to put it in the dishwasher. Place the china in a cold oven, and set the temperature to gas mark

2/3, 300/325°F (150/170°C). Bake for 30-35 minutes, timing from when the oven temperature stabilizes at the desired level.

2 Turn off the oven when finished and leave the china to cool slowly in the oven. There may be a slight odour during baking but this is non-toxic and harmless.

Sunflower

Cut out the sunflower centre

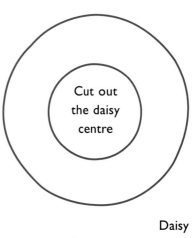

Cut out the daisy centre

Daisy

Make tracings of these flower motifs to transfer the outlines on to your china.

Painted Flower Pots

Traditionally ceramic painting is done on fired china, with a non-porous surface. Now, by using a special filler paint as an undercoat, it is possible to paint on almost any fired china, even porous surfaces like flower pots. Use the decorated pots as plant holders; or to hold fruit, kitchen utensils or pencils

Make sure that the terracotta pots are dust free and completely dry before painting: if necessary place in a warm oven to remove excess moisture before painting.

You will need

- Terracotta flower pots
- Water-based porcelain paint – tangerine, light brown, olive green, clay green, bright yellow, emerald, coral, ruby, charcoal, ming blue, powder blue, orange, ivory
- Porcelain outliner – dark green, plum, dark grey, ming blue, pewter
- Filler undercoat
- Matt medium
- Selection of paintbrushes
- Tracing paper, masking tape
- Typewriter carbon paper, pencil, ball-point pen
- Container of water, kitchen paper
- Palette, damp cloth

Transferring the design

1 Trace the motifs on page 23 on to tracing paper using a pencil. Using masking tape, secure a piece of carbon paper, shiny side down, to the side of the flower pot. Secure the tracing over the carbon paper, and then, using a ball-point pen, carefully draw over the design lines.

Painting the fruit design

1 Paint over the fruit motif shape using a single coat of filler undercoat: this will act as a primer and prevents the pot soaking up the paint. Paint just the motif shape, leaving the rest of the pot untouched. Allow at least 2 hours drying time before moving on to the next step.

2 Apply 2-3 coats of ivory paint over the filler-coated fruit, building up an even layer of paint; allow to dry between coats.

3 Outline the fruit shapes, and add detail lines to the fruit and leaves, using dark green outliner: squeeze the tube gently as if using an icing tube. Allow the outliner to dry before continuing. Do not paint on any areas of unprimed pot.

4 Using a little clay green and lime green, paint the base of the pear: the lime green is made by mixing emerald and bright yellow

together. Paint should be applied heavily to create a 'pool' of colour, allowing it to run unchecked up to the outlines. Colours within the design should run into each other, creating an interesting mixed effect. Fill the remainder of the pear with a thick 'pool' of bright yellow and orange paint; add tangerine and a little light brown to give shading. Allow the paint colours to mix together and flow up to the outlines.

5 Paint the apple in the same way, using green shades at the top, and coral and ruby at the sides and base. Paint clay green and lime green on the leaves. Leave to dry for at least 7 days before hardening.

Painting the poppies

1 Paint the flower pot with one coat of filler undercoat. For a neat top, put a ring of masking tape around the inside rim of the pot, then paint up to the tape.

2 When the filler is completely dry, paint over it using the ivory paint. It will take several coats of ivory to obtain a solid even finish. Allow plenty of drying time between coats; and clean the base of the pot with a damp cloth to remove runs. When baked the ivory paint will change from off white to ivory.

3 When the ivory is dry, transfer the poppy design on page 23 to the side of the pot.

4 Outline the poppies using plum outliner, with dark green for the leaves and bud. Do not outline the poppy centre at this stage.

5 Paint the poppy flowers by filling the area with a deep 'pool' of colour; use ruby next to the flower centre, coral towards the middle and tangerine towards the edges. Paint the poppy centres using lime green. Apply clay green and lime green to the leaves and bud.

6 Leave to dry for 1-2 hours before applying dark grey outliner to the poppy centres. A border pattern can be added to the pot top at this stage.

Adding border patterns

1 Double lines – Paint the border at the top by placing the flower pot on a cake decorating turntable, or on an upside-down pudding basin covered with cling-film. To paint a straight line around the pot top: load the brush with paint (coral or ruby) then hold the tip against the pot. Turn the turntable or basin slowly, while keeping the brush against the pot. Do not move the brush, but keep it in the same position until the line has been completed. Re-apply if necessary to give a thicker line.

2 Checked top – Apply a thin strip of masking tape around the middle of the pot top. Using a stencil brush, paint around the pot above and below the tape; allow to dry before removing the tape. Apply strips of tape vertically around the pot, between the painted lines; allow to dry before removing the tape.

Painting the blue mosaic

1 Put masking tape around the inside rim of the pot, then paint the pot up to the tape with filler undercoat. When dry, paint with a base coat of ivory.

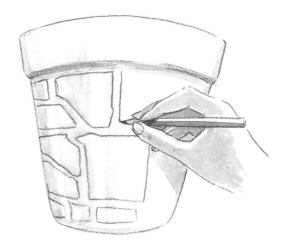

2 With a soft pencil and using the template on page 23 as a guide, draw shapes around the pot. Make a ring of smaller shapes around the rim.

3 Using ming blue outliner draw over the outlines of the mosaic 'pieces'.

4 When the outliner is dry, fill the centre of each shape with a deep pool of colour, allowing the paint to spread up to the outlines. Use a variety of colours, painting roughly half the 'pieces' in the blue shades. Paint some pieces with simple patterns of stripes and spots; or paint pieces with a pale colour, adding stripes when dry.

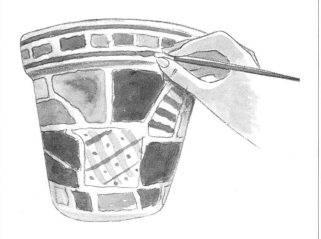

5 Decorate the top of the pot with lines of blue paint either side of the mosaic ring, following instructions on the previous page for adding border patterns.

Painting the sand mosaic

1 Paint the pot with the filler undercoat, up to the top of the pot.

2 When thoroughly dry, mix the 'sand' colour using light brown, ivory and bright yellow. Apply 2-3 coats, taking it up to the top of the pot; wipe off any excess paint.

3 When dry, apply one coat of matt medium to the pot, then allow to dry. This will give the paint a matt effect when baked. Matt medium can also be added to the paint, but this can turn streaky when baked unless several coats are applied.

4 With a soft pencil and using the template on page 23 as a guide, draw shapes around the pot and smaller pieces on the rim.

5 Using the pewter outliner, draw around the mosaic 'pieces'; when dry fill with colour.

Drying the pots

1 As these pots have many coats of paint, allow to dry for 7 days before baking; insufficient drying time will result in the paint bubbling as it is heated.

Hardening the pots

1 It is necessary to thermoharden water-based porcelain paint in a domestic oven. Place the pots in a cold oven, and set the temperature to gas mark 2/3, 300/325°F (150/170°C). Bake for 30-35 minutes, timing from when the oven temperature stabilizes at the desired level. Turn the oven off when finished and leave the pots to cool completely before removing.

Poppy Pot

Fruit Pot

Mosaic Pot

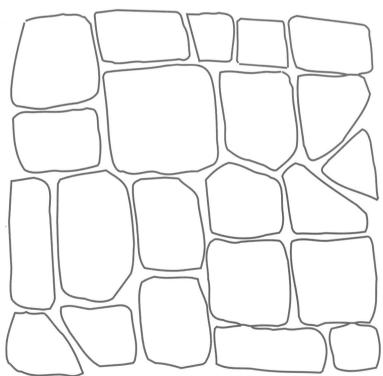

Use this key and the coloured
diagrams on the previous page
for painting the pots; refer to
the project instructions for
painting the outlines.

Key to Colours

 Ruby

 Coral

 Orange/Tangerine

Lime

 Clay Green

 Bright Yellow

Art Deco Cruet Set

Soft muted shades of mauve, yellow and green have been used to paint
a cruet set in the style of Clarice Cliff. This pretty yet functional cruet
carefully combines bold circular and angular shapes, bringing colour,
cheer and the art deco period to your dining table

To complete this design, choose a plain cruet
set with flat surfaces and straight sides.
Although some of the design can be traced on
to the china, a certain amount of freehand
drawing is included in this project.

You will need
- White china cruet set
- White china cruet tray
- Water-based porcelain paint – orange, sage
  green, deep lilac, dark grey, yellow
- Small paintbrushes
- White paper, typewriter carbon paper
- Pencil, masking tape
- Chinagraph pencil, ball-point pen
- Container of water, kitchen paper
- Alcohol, cloth, cotton bud

Preparing the china
1 Wash the china in warm soapy water and
dry thoroughly.

2 Using kitchen paper, wipe the surface of the
china with alcohol, then leave to dry: the
alcohol will remove any greasy marks and help
the paint to adhere to the surface of the china.

Transferring the design
1 Lay white paper over the tree and hill
design on page 27. Trace over the designs
carefully using a soft pencil. You can use a
photocopier if you need to enlarge or reduce
the size of the design to fit your tray.

2 To transfer the design: cut a piece of carbon
paper just larger than the design. Attach
the carbon paper shiny side down on to the
china using masking tape. Place the tracing on
top of the carbon. Carefully go over the design
lines with a ball-point pen, pressing hard
enough to ensure a good transfer.

Painting the tray
1 Using a medium paintbrush, paint the
outer and inner rim of the tray with orange
porcelain paint, leave to dry. The paint should
be touch dry in about 10 minutes.

2 Fill in the background area of the tray with
one coat of yellow paint.

3 Paint the trees and hills using deep lilac and yellow, and the trunks sage green; wash your brushes in water and dry on kitchen paper between each colour. Make sure that any adjoining, already painted areas are dry, so that the colours do not run together. Use thin coats, and allow to dry for at least 10 minutes, before applying another coat.

4 Paint the flowers and leaves using deep lilac, orange and green; leave to dry.

5 Using a fine paintbrush, outline the sections with dark grey paint.

Painting the cruet set

1 Make tracings of the plant and flower designs on page 27, and transfer them to the top and bottom of the salt and pepper pot, using carbon paper; or draw the design freehand using a chinagraph pencil. Draw a hill shape around the pot joining one side of the plant to the other.

2 Draw co-ordinating patterns on the vinegar and oil bottles using a chinagraph pencil: take your inspiration from the tray design,

drawing curved tree trunks and angular shapes, and incorporate the handles into the design. Add a smaller flower to the bottle lids.

3 Paint the cruet set using the same colours as on the tray: use one coat for the background, and two for the design.

4 When the paint is dry, outline the painted sections on the cruet set using a fine paintbrush and dark grey paint.

Drying time

1 Allow the paint to dry for a full 48 hours before hardening: if the paint has been applied thickly allow a longer drying time.

Hardening the paint

1 It is necessary to thermoharden water-based porcelain paint in a domestic oven to make it strong enough to stand up to normal use in the kitchen, although it would be advisable not to put it in the dishwasher. Place the cruet set in a cold oven, and set the temperature to gas mark 2/3, 300/325°F (150/170°C). Bake for 30-35 minutes, timing from when the oven temperature stabilizes at the desired level. Turn off the oven when finished and leave to cool slowly in the oven.

Tree and Hill Tray Design

Flower Design

Make tracings of these art deco designs to transfer the outlines on to your china.

Plant Design

Maritime Tiles

Make your study into a seaside retreat with these handpainted tiles featuring a windswept sea scene. Worked in shades of blue, the scene of a windswept headland, boats and a lighthouse can be used individually, or together to create a nautical frieze on a notice board or tray

To use as a coaster, glue green baize or felt to the underside of the tile.

You will need

- White ceramic tiles – two 15x15cm (6x6in) and four 11x11cm (4¼x4¼in)
- Water-based porcelain paint – ultramarine blue, ivory
- Gloss medium
- Small, medium paintbrushes
- White paper, pencil, acetate, stiff card
- Typewriter carbon paper, plastic bag
- Ball-point pen, cocktail stick, flat dish for mixing paint
- Compass, scissors, craft knife, cutting mat
- Container of water, kitchen paper, sponge
- Alcohol, cloth, cotton bud, jam jar

Transferring the design

1 Wipe over the tiles using clean soapy water, then dry using kitchen paper. Clean the tiles with alcohol to remove any oily deposits: this will enable the paint to adhere to the surface of the tile properly. Allow to dry thoroughly before painting.

2 Trace over the designs for the small tiles on pages 32 and 33 on to white paper, then cut out the tile design. Cut a square of typewriter carbon paper to the same size, and lay it, shiny side down, on top of the tile. Place the tracing on top, then carefully draw over the design lines with a ball-point pen.

Applying the paint

1 The ultramarine blue paint is used neat; mixed with ivory to produce a whiter shade of blue; or lightened with gloss medium to produce a lighter tone of the same colour without thinning the consistency of the paint (see Painting Techniques, page 9). A blend of ⅓ medium with ⅔ colour can be mixed without reducing the colour adherence.

Painting the boat tiles

1 Mix a little gloss medium with the blue paint in a flat dish to provide a lighter shade; do not mix too much paint at any one time as the paint dries quickly. Using a medium paintbrush apply a coat of mixed blue

to the sails and boat hulls. Build up the layers, allowing the paint to dry between coats. If you apply a second coat before the first one is dry, the paint may pull off.

2 To paint the sea area, apply a slightly thicker coat of blue paint straight from the bottle; any brush strokes will be hidden when you apply the 'bagging' effect to the paint. To do this, scrunch a very small piece of plastic bag into a ball, then, while the paint is still wet, carefully emphasise the crest of the waves by pouncing the scrunched plastic on and off the paint. Practice 'bagging' on a spare tile until you feel confident enough to try the technique on your tile, (see Painting Techniques, page 11). Do not apply the paint too thickly or you will have difficulty in

achieving the desired effect. Allow to dry for 10 minutes before continuing.

3 Take a small piece of sponge and moisten it with water; press the sponge on to kitchen paper to remove the excess water. On a plate, mix ivory paint with a small amount of blue, until you have a pale blue colour; then apply with long brush strokes to the sky area of the tile. Whilst the paint is still wet, use the damp sponge to remove small areas, forming clouds. Leave to dry for at least 48 hours.

Painting the lighthouse tile

1 Mix blue paint with the gloss medium, as before. Using a fine paintbrush, paint the outline of the lighthouse, then fill in the alternate stripes, roof and leaded viewing area.

2 Paint the sea, sky and clouds in the same way as for the boat tile; allow the paint to dry for 30 minutes before scratching off the seagulls and the lighthouse windows with a cocktail stick (see Painting Techniques, page 10). Leave to dry for at least 48 hours.

Painting the coastline tile

1 Mix blue with the gloss medium, then paint the foreland and house fronts. The house roofs are painted in one coat of blue, straight from the bottle; the background hills are painted in two coats of blue. Allow to dry for 10 minutes between coats.

2 Paint the sea, sky and clouds as before, then leave to dry for 30 minutes before scratching off the seagulls, the windows shapes, and the chimney smoke with a cocktail stick. Leave to dry for at least 48 hours.

Painting the large tiles

1 Cut a piece of stiff card the same size as the larger tile. Using a compass, draw a 11cm (4¼in) circle in the centre of the square. Carefully cut out the circle with either scissors or a craft knife. Place the square over the tile and draw inside the circle with a pencil; this will give an outline for your chosen scene.

2 Using a tracing and carbon paper, apply your design to the tile as before. If any of the design lines go outside the circle, remove them with kitchen paper.

3 Paint the centre of the tile, keeping within the circle. Leave to dry.

4 Cut a square of acetate 4x4cm (1½x1½in). Lay the acetate over the anchor on page 32, putting the point of the acetate into the 90° angle, shown by a dotted line. Using a ball-point pen, trace over the anchor outline.

Carefully cut out the anchor shape, using a craft knife and cutting mat.

5 To sponge the anchor: pick up a small amount of blue paint on to a damp sponge, and dab the excess paint off on to kitchen paper. Place the stencil on the tile, positioning the point of the acetate into one corner; hold the stencil in place with masking tape. Liberally sponge blue paint into the cut-out area of the stencil. Lift off, clean and reposition the stencil in the other corners. Leave to dry for at least 48 hours.

Hardening your design

1 It is necessary to thermoharden water-based porcelain paint in a domestic oven to make it strong enough to stand up to normal use. Place the tiles in a cold oven, and set the temperature to gas mark 2/3, 300/325°F (150/170°C). Bake for 30-35 minutes, timing from when the oven temperature stabilizes at the desired level. As the paint has been applied fairly thinly to the tiles, it is very important that the oven temperature and baking time is exact or the colours may darken; harden all the tiles together so that they receive the same amount of hardening time. Turn the oven off when finished, and leave the tiles to cool completely before removing.

Anchor Stencil
Put the 90° angle shown by the dotted line into one corner of the tile.

Lighthouse

Make tracings from these designs to transfer the outlines on to the tiles

Large Boat

Small Boat

Coastline

Freehand Painted Mugs

These stylish mugs can be completed in just a few hours using a simple freestyle paint technique. By choosing coloured mugs, painting time can be saved, and only one coat of paint will be needed to create the design. This is a great starter project, as only a minimum of equipment and paint colours are needed

To save painting time, use coloured mugs for this project. If you are using white mugs, they will need to be painted with three coats of pale lemon paint before decorating.

You will need
- Plain coloured ceramic mugs
- Water-based porcelain paint – coral, bottle green, deep yellow, ming blue
- White paper, double-sided tape, scissors
- Small piece of sponge
- Small, medium paintbrushes
- Flat dish for mixing paint
- Alcohol, water, kitchen paper

Preparing the china

1 Wash the mugs in warm soapy water and dry thoroughly.

2 Using kitchen paper, wipe the surface of the china with alcohol, then leave to dry: the alcohol will remove any greasy marks and help the paint adhere to the surface of the china.

Using porcelain paint

1 When using a freehand technique try to keep the thickness of the paint even. As this design uses only one coat of paint, brush marks cannot be avoided; they can be reduced by using a natural hair brush. When painting freestyle, mistakes are easy to make: wipe the wet paint away using moist kitchen paper, or a cotton bud; if the mug has been left to dry, scrubbing with warm water may be necessary to remove the paint.

Painting the stripey mug

1 Decide roughly how many lines you can fit around your mug; this will depend on the size of the mug and the brushes you are using.

2 In a flat dish mix together bottle green, deep yellow and coral paint to give a dark sage green colour. With the mug balanced in the palm of one hand, and holding the paintbrush in the other, paint a continuous line around the mug starting and finishing at the

handle, taking care not to smudge the paint as you move around the mug. If the paint is too thick, water-based paint can be diluted with up to 10% water (see Painting Techniques, page 9); however using over this amount may reduce the adherence.

3 Continue painting rings around the mug using the mixed dark sage green, coral and ming blue paint. Change the size of the paintbrushes to give a variety of line widths. Leave the mug to dry for a few minutes between rings to avoided smudges.

Painting the floral mug

1 Decide how many flowers you can fit around your mug, then cut circles from white paper using the floral mug trace on page 37 as a guide. Using double-sided tape, attach the paper circles around the mug, alternating the height to give tall and short flowers.

2 Pour dark sage green paint into a flat dish, then dip a dry sponge into the paint. Dab the paint quite heavily around the bottom 1cm (1/2in) of the mug to give the impression of grass. Using a smaller amount of paint on the sponge, add the grassy spikes by dabbing lightly above the grass area.

3 Using the dark sage green and a medium paintbrush, paint the flower stalks and leaves between the paper circles and the grass.

4 Remove the paper circles from the mug; then, using ming blue and coral, paint swirls at the top of each stalk. Start the swirl just above the stalk and then progress inwards to the centre in a single movement.

Painting the spiral spots

1 Cut out eight circles of white paper using the spiral spots trace on page 37. Using

double-sided tape stick these randomly over the surface of the mug.

2 Pour dark sage green paint into a flat dish, then dip the sponge into the paint. Dab the sponge over the surface of the mug, adding more paint as the colour begins to weaken. The sponge should be pressed quite firmly on to the surface of the china to give a dense covering: do not paint the handle. Allow the paint to dry for about 15 minutes before carefully removing the paper circles.

3 Paint spirals on the unpainted circles using a medium paintbrush. Start at the centre of each spiral, working outwards in a continuous stroke using ming blue and coral paint.

Painting the chequered mug

1 Paint diagonal stripes from top to bottom, and left to right, around the mug using dark sage green paint. Using the same colours, cross the lines in the opposite direction to form diamond shapes. As the design is freehand, do not worry if the diamonds are different sizes.

2 With a small paintbrush add coral spirals to the centre of each diamond, starting at the centre and working out.

3 Add a line of ming blue paint inside each diamond, using a small paintbrush.

Drying time

1 Allow the paint to air dry for a full 48 hours before hardening. Bubbling may occur during hardening if the paint is not completely dry.

Hardening the mug

1 It is necessary to thermoharden water-based porcelain paint in a domestic oven to make it strong enough to stand up to normal use in the kitchen, although it would be advisable not to put the china in the dishwasher. Place the mugs in a cold oven, and set the temperature to gas mark 2/3, 300/325°F (150/170°C). Bake for 30-35 minutes, timing from when the oven temperature stabilizes at the desired level.

2 Turn the oven off when finished and leave to cool completely before removing the mugs from the oven.

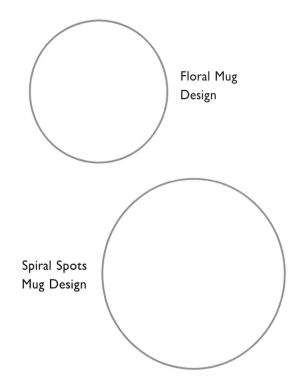

Floral Mug Design

Spiral Spots Mug Design

Use these circular templates as guides when painting spirals on your mugs.

Finger Painted Teapots

If you have never painted china before, then here's an ideal first project: painted in pastel shades of pink and blue, each teapot can easily be completed in an evening. Simply dab the paint on to the teapot using your finger wrapped in an old piece of towelling

You will need to prime each piece of towelling before using. To do this: wrap a piece of towelling around your index finger, then dip it in the paint. Leave the primed towelling to dry before reloading with paint ready for use.

You will need

- White china tea pot
- White china mug
- Water-based porcelain paint – coral, dark green, deep yellow, powder blue, sapphire blue, peacock blue
- Terry towelling
- Alcohol, kitchen paper
- Flat plate for mixing paints

Painting the teapots

1 Wash the teapots in warm soapy water and dry thoroughly. Wipe the surface of the china with alcohol to remove greasy marks.

2 To paint the pink teapot: after priming, wrap the towelling around your finger and dip it in the coral paint. Dab and dot your finger on to the china every half inch or so. Reapply paint every two or three dabs.

3 Mix dark green with coral to make red brown. Prime a fresh piece of towelling, then dab the paint on to the china. Repeat with the yellow and then the dark green.

4 Dip your finger into two or three of the paint colours and fill any remaining areas of white china. Leave to dry for 15 minutes, then repeat for a deeper finish.

5 For the blue pot: use powder blue mixed with sapphire; sapphire; sapphire mixed with peacock blue; and finally peacock blue.

Hardening the teapots

1 Leave the painted china to dry for at least 48 hours. Place in a cold oven, then set the temperature to gas mark 2/3, 300/325°F (150/170°C). Bake for 30-35 minutes, timing from when the oven temperature stabilizes. Turn off the oven and leave to cool.

French Tiles

Just imagine fields of sunflowers, lavender and grapes ripening under clear blue skies. Bring a little Provencal sunshine into your kitchen with these rustic tiles inspired by the French countryside. Dotted around your worktops they are sure to bring a taste of the good life into your home

If you would like to paint these designs on to a different size of tile, use a photocopier to enlarge or reduce the designs to fit.

You will need
- White ceramic tiles – 15x15cm (6x6in)
- Water-based porcelain paint – bronze, bright yellow, deep yellow, orange, bright green, brown, ivory, sapphire blue, purple
- Porcelain outliner – copper, dark grey, pewter
- Small paintbrushes
- Flat plate for mixing paint
- White paper, masking tape
- Typewriter carbon paper, pencil
- Container of water, kitchen paper
- Alcohol, cloth, cotton bud

Transferring the design

1 Wipe over the tiles using clean soapy water; dry using kitchen paper.

2 Clean the tiles with alcohol to remove any oily deposits: this will enable the paint to adhere to the surface of the tile properly. Allow to dry thoroughly.

3 Lay white paper over the tile templates on pages 46, 47, 48 and 49. Trace over the designs carefully using a soft pencil. Tape a piece of carbon paper shiny side down over the tile, then secure a tracing in the centre of the tile with masking tape. Carefully draw over the lines with a ball-point pen, pressing hard enough to ensure a good transfer. When you have traced over the lines, remove the paper and the carbon from the tile.

Painting the tiles

1 The French tiles should be painted in a free style that resembles an oil painting: to do this some adjoining colours should be added while the paint is tacky, but not wet. This will make the different areas of colour less defined, blending the edges of the colours together. In some areas, colours need to be mixed together on the tile: this will give a mottled semi-mixed effect to the paint. If colours need to be dried between applications, drying time will depend on the thickness of the paint, but it should be

approximately 10 minutes. A hairdryer will accelerate this process (see Painting Techniques, page 13). If you make a mistake while painting it can easily be wiped away using moist kitchen paper. If the piece has been left to dry for a long time, scrubbing with warm water may be necessary.

Painting the sunflower field

1 Make a tracing of the sunflower design on page 49 and transfer it on to the centre of your tile.

2 Using a medium paintbrush, paint the border edge around the design with bronze coloured paint. Leave to dry.

3 Using deep yellow paint make circular shapes for the sunflower heads; add a few flower heads in bright yellow as a contrast. While the paint is still tacky, randomly blob small amounts of bright green between the flower heads.

4 Apply two coats of sapphire blue to the sky area, leaving to dry between coats.

5 The main area of the field behind the flowers is painted in deep yellow with a bright green shadow in the centre; when dry add detail lines to the field using brown paint. For the distant hills, blend bright green and brown together on the tile.

6 Paint the tree trunks using bronze paint; leave to dry before giving a second coat.

7 Fill in the tree tops using bright green paint; leave to dry. Vary the colour of the trees by painting several more coats over some parts of the tree tops: use different shades of green, mixing bright green with varying proportions of deep yellow. Leave the paint to dry between coats. Finally add shading to the leaves using touches of dark brown and ivory.

8 Use the tube of copper outliner to draw in the tree trunks.

9 Using a fine paintbrush, make a brown circle in the centre of each sunflower head, and outline each flower with a circle of small dots: flowers in the foreground should be more defined then those in the background. When the paint is dry, paint over some of the flower centres to make them darker.

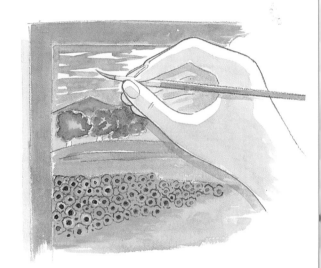

10 Use ivory paint in streaks across the sky area of the design, forming clouds.

11 Finally, apply another two coats of bronze around the border edge, leaving to dry between coats.

12 Leave the tile to air dry for at least a week, before hardening in the oven. Bubbling may occur during hardening if the paint is not completely dry.

Painting the church

1 Make a tracing of the church design on page 47 and transfer it to your tile.

2 Paint the border edge around the design with a coat of bright yellow paint; leave to dry completely before continuing.

3 In a dish, mix a little bright yellow with brown to make a light brown colour. Roughly paint the church buildings, leaving some areas of white tile showing through; leave to dry.

4 Paint the front grass areas of the tile using a very thin layer of bright green mixed with a small amount of bright yellow; leave to dry.

5 Paint the hills in the distance with bright green lightened with bright yellow; while still tacky use brown to shade, adding more shading to the hill on the left hand side of the tile. Leave to dry.

6 Using a thin brush, add shading to the walls and the rooftops using brown; brown mixed with ivory; and orange. Leave to dry.

7 Use brown paint to define the edges of the roof, the walls and to paint the windows.

8 Paint the tall tree in the centre of the tile using bright green and leave to dry. Give the tree a second coat, shading the left side with brown; for the other trees and bushes use bright green and bright green mixed with bright yellow and/or brown, leaving drying time between each coat. Use the darkest colour last, dabbing the paint on to the trees and bushes to give a mottled effect.

9 Paint the sky in sapphire blue; when dry streak with ivory to form the clouds.

10 Using a thin brush, lightly paint the grass at the front of the tile in bright green and brown paint; leave to dry.

11 Paint the flower stems using a thick coat of bright green paint, and the flowers in ivory. When dry add small brown dots to the centre of each flower.

12 Add a second layer of bright yellow to the border, leaving to dry between coats.

13 Leave the tile to air dry for at least a week before hardening.

Painting the chateau

1 Make a tracing of the chateau design on page 46 and transfer it on to the centre of your tile.

2 Paint the border edge around the design using bright yellow paint; leave to dry.

3 Beginning with the chateau, paint the triangular roof with a thin layer of brown; wait for the paint to get tacky then draw horizontal orange and brown lines across the roof, adding ivory lines for highlights.

4 Paint the walls using a thin layer of brown, then, when dry, add patches of orange and ivory. Add detail lines in brown and copper outliner; leave to dry.

5 The chateau windows are painted in orange; when dry use copper outliner to define the top window edges and brown outlines along the bottom.

6 The buildings at the top of the tile are painted using orange for the roofs, with a thin coat of brown on the walls. The chimneys are painted in ivory.

7 Paint over the sky area using sapphire blue, blended with a little ivory. The top of the sky should be darker than the bottom.

8 The river is also painted using sapphire blue: build up the layers leaving drying time between coats. This will give darker areas of river near the chateau, on the left-hand side, and in the centre. When dry, use white to add detail, subtly at the top and with thicker streaks at the bottom.

9 Use a medium paintbrush to dab a light coat of bright green paint on to the bushes. While the paint is still tacky, add patches of the same bright green, and shades of green made up by mixing bright green with brown and ivory. Make brush strokes in different directions over the bushes to give a leafy effect. Use a small paintbrush to add brown to the path at the bottom of the tile and to paint along the top river bank.

10 When the paint is completely dry, dot copper outliner on the edge of the tall tree on the left side of the tile. Using pewter outliner, draw around the buildings and bushes at the top of the tile, and add railings to the chateau windows.

11 Using a medium paintbrush, add two more layers of bright yellow paint to the border edge, leaving to dry between coats.

12 Leave the tile to dry for at least a week before hardening.

Painting the lavender field

1 Make a tracing of the lavender field design on page 48 and transfer it on to the centre of your tile.

2 Paint the border edge around the lavender field using bronze paint; leave to dry.

3 Using bright green, paint a thin layer over the fields, hills and trees. Paint a second coat of bright green along the top of the hills, with brown along the bottom, allowing the colours to merge together; leave to dry.

4 On the tree, paint a second layer of bright green and brown, again allowing the colours to merge together; add ivory to the top left of the tree.

5 Paint faint lines of dark brown between the rows of lavender; leave to dry. Paint the lavender heads using tiny blobs of purple paint between the brown lines.

6 When the paint is dry, use brown for the tree trunk and bright green and ivory for the row of bushes between the field and the hills beyond.

7 Use copper outliner to draw wobbly lines between the rows of lavender over the thin brown lines. With a fine paintbrush, draw tiny dots of ivory paint over the lavender dots.

8 Fill in the sky with sapphire blue paint, blending it downwards – darker at the top adding white as you move towards the bottom. Leave the paint to dry, then add streaky clouds using ivory paint in the same way as for the sunflower tile.

9 Add two more layers of bronze to the border edge, leaving to dry between coats. Leave the tile to air dry for at least a week before hardening.

Hardening the tiles

1 As the paint has been applied thickly, allow the tiles to air dry for at least a week before hardening. Bubbling may occur on the surface of the tile during the hardening if the paint is not completely dry.

2 It is necessary to thermoharden water-based porcelain paint in a domestic oven to make it strong enough to stand up to normal use. Place the tiles in a cold oven, and set the temperature to gas mark 2/3, 300/325°F

To make the French tiles into coasters, glue green baize or felt to the underside of the tiles.

(150/170°C). Bake for 30-35 minutes, timing from when the oven temperature stabilizes at the desired level.

3 Turn the oven off when finished and leave to cool completely before removing the tiles from the oven.

4 Fix the tiles to the wall using tile adhesive; grout around the tiles carefully, removing any splashes from the tiles before they dry. Do not use painted tiles in a shower cubicle, or in areas of heavy usage. When cleaning, do not use scouring powder as it can remove the paint.

Painting the Chateau

Border edge – bright yellow

Chateau roof – brown and orange, brown detail lines and ivory highlights

Walls – brown with patches of orange and ivory, detail lines in brown and copper outliner

Windows – orange with copper outliner along the top edges, brown along the bottom; railings in pewter outliner

Far buildings – orange roofs, brown walls, chimneys ivory, outlined in pewter outliner

Sky – sapphire blue, streaked with ivory

River – sapphire blue with ivory detail

Bushes and trees – bright green paint and shades of green; rear bushes outlined in pewter outliner; dot copper outliner on the edge of the tall tree

Path and top river bank – brown

Painting the Church

Border – bright yellow paint

Church – roughly painted in light brown; detail in brown, brown mixed with ivory, and orange

Grass – bright green mixed with bright yellow; detail in bright green and brown

Hills in the distance – bright green lightened with bright yellow, brown for shading

Trees – tall tree in bright green, shaded on the left side with brown; other trees and bushes in bright green and bright green mixed with bright yellow and or brown

Sky – sapphire blue streaked with ivory

Flower stems – bright green

Flowers – ivory with brown centres

Painting the Lavender Field
Border edge – bronze
Fields and hills – bright green and brown
Tree – bright green and brown with ivory
highlights
Tree trunk – brown
Bushes – bright green and ivory
Lavender – faint lines in dark brown between the
rows, over painted with copper outliner; lavender
flowers, purple dotted with ivory
Sky – sapphire blue with clouds in ivory

Painting the Sunflower Field
Border edge – bronze
Sunflower heads – deep yellow and bright yellow, with bright green between
Sunflower centres – brown
Sunflower outlines – brown dots
Sky – sapphire blue streaked with ivory
Rear field – deep yellow with bright green shadows; detail lines in brown
Distant hills – bright green and brown
Tree trunks – bronze, outlined in copper outliner
Trees tops – bright green and shades of green, detail in dark brown and ivory

Malachite Coffee Set

Green, blue and gold paint have been used to create a malachite effect on this plain white coffee set. Use for everyday entertaining; or add a few decorations, bright napkins and a spoonful of festive cheer, and you will have a set of china that can also be used at the Christmas table

Malachite is a marble-like, copper based mineral which is highly polished and used for making ornaments.

You will need

- White china saucers, coffee cups and dessert plates
- Water-based porcelain paint – olive green, gold, bottle green, dark green, ming blue, turquoise
- Porcelain outliner – gold
- 1.2cm (½in) wide masking tape, scissors
- Fan paintbrush
- Container of water, kitchen paper
- Alcohol, cloth

Preparing the china

1 Wash the china in warm soapy water and dry thoroughly.

2 Using kitchen paper, wipe the surface of the china with alcohol, then leave to dry: the alcohol will help the paint adhere to the china.

Painting the malachite effect

1 Before you begin painting the coffee set, practise making the malachite effect on a white tile or old piece of china. Using a fan paintbrush, apply swirls to the china in a tight circular movement. Keep the brush almost vertical and the bristles in contact with the china to provide a continuous flow of paint; make crimps in some of the swirls to give a ripple effect. The first swirls should be positioned so that they are just touching, but not overlapping (see Painting Techniques, page 12).

2 Before the paint dries, make more swirls in two different colours, in the gaps between and overlapping the first swirls (see diagrams on page 53). Use gold paint very lightly over the top of the swirls, using the same brush movement as for the other colours; in some areas the gold paint should hardly be visible. As the paint is not water-resistant until fired, if you make a mistake wash off the paint, dry, then wipe over with alcohol before re-painting.

Painting the saucer

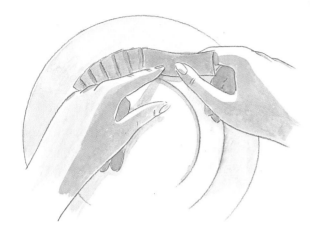

1 Carefully pleat masking tape following the inner edge of the rim of the saucer; if necessary draw a circle, using a chinagraph pencil, to use as a guide for the tape. Dip the fan paintbrush in the olive green paint; then, holding the brush almost horizontal, make swirls around the saucer rim: make about five ring segments around the saucer edge.

2 Before the paint dries, make swirls using the dark green and then the bottle green paint in the gaps between the first rings. Repeat the process over the top of the green swirls using gold. Leave the paint to touch dry before removing the masking tape.

Painting the cup

1 Using masking tape, create a scalloped border edge around the top of the cup. If the cup has a raised border edge, this can be used as an outline for the tape; if the cup is plain, divide the rim into sixths, then apply the tape in a curve within each division. Fix a length of masking tape around the inner top edge of the cup to give a neat finish.

2 Apply paint to the cup using the same method as for the saucer.

3 When touch dry, peel off the masking tape, then add a dot of gold outliner paint to each scallop point.

Painting the plate

1 Fix masking tape along the inner edge of the rim of the plate, in the same way as the saucer. Mask off the outer rim, snipping the tape so that it curves smoothly into scallops.

2 Apply the malachite effect to the plate rim using the same method as for the saucer. Start with the olive green paint, then apply ming blue and turquoise rings; finish with gold. When the paint is touch dry, peel off the masking tape.

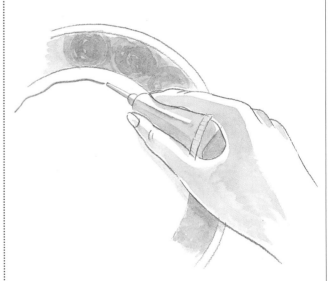

3 Use gold outliner paint to make a simple pattern on the outer edge of the plate. If your china has a raised border decoration, use this as a pattern for the paint. Make a wavy line of gold outliner just inside the inner decorated rim.

Drying time

1 Allow the paint to air dry for a full 48 hours before hardening: if the paint has been applied thickly allow a longer drying

The gold outlines were painted following the raised border decorations on the plates.

time. Bubbling may occur during hardening if the paint is not completely dry.

Hardening the paint

1 It is necessary to thermoharden water-based porcelain paint in a domestic oven to make it strong enough to stand up to normal use in the kitchen, although it would be advisable not to put it in the dishwasher. Place the china in a cold oven, and set the temperature to gas mark 2/3, 300/325°F (150/170°C). Bake for 30-35 minutes, timing from when the oven temperature stabilizes at the desired level.

2 Turn the oven off when finished and leave to cool completely before removing the china from the oven. There may be some odour from the baking china but this is non-toxic.

Painting the Mosaic Effect

1 Using a fan paintbrush, apply swirls to the china in a tight circular movement. Keep the brush almost vertical, and the bristles in contact with the china. Position the first swirls so that they are just touching without overlapping.

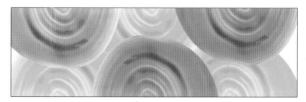

2 Before the paint dries, make more swirls in two different colours using the same brush movement as before. Paint in the gaps between and overlapping the first swirls.

Mediterranean Bowls

There can be no nicer way to serve your summer salads than in these bright hand-painted bowls. Inspired by the colours of the Mediterranean, the broad stripes of yellow and blue have been over-painted with olives and sprigs of herbs, to recreate all the warmth and taste of a continental evening

This design can be applied to any plain white china, by adjusting the spacing between the traces to fit the rim of your bowls. If you are using the bowls for food, keep the design mainly around the rim, as the paint can be scratched by cutlery.

You will need
- White china bowls
- Water-based porcelain paint – deep yellow, charcoal, royal blue, amber, orange, leaf green
- Small, medium paintbrushes
- Small decorator's paintbrush
- White paper, glue stick, masking tape
- Typewriter carbon paper, pencil
- Chinagraph pencil, ball-point pen
- Tape measure, scissors
- Container of water, kitchen paper
- Alcohol, cloth, cotton bud, jam jar

Preparing the bowls
1 Wash the bowls in warm soapy water and dry thoroughly.

2 Using kitchen paper, wipe the surface of the china with alcohol, then leave to dry: the alcohol will help the paint adhere to the china.

Transferring the design
1 Lay white paper over the bowl motifs on page 57. Trace the designs carefully using a soft pencil. You can use a photocopier if you prefer not to mark your book, or if you need to enlarge or reduce the size of the motifs to fit your bowls.

2 Measure the circumference of your bowl. Divide the measurement into quarters, marking the divisions on the china using a chinagraph pencil. On the large bowl, the three olives and the sprig of foliage have been painted within each quarter section of the bowl; on the smaller bowl, two sprig stems are painted within each quarter. Enlarge or reduce the distance between the pattern repeats at the quarter marks to fit around your bowls.

3 Cut a piece of carbon paper the same size as the tracing; using a glue stick, attach the carbon paper, shiny side up, to the tracing. Using masking tape, stick the tracing to the bowl with the carbon paper shiny side against

the china. Carefully go over the design lines with a ball-point pen, pressing hard enough to ensure good transfer. Re-position the tracing and repeat the pattern in the four quarters of the bowl.

Using porcelain paint

1 Apply the paint in thin coats, leaving the paint to dry between each. Mistakes can be wiped away easily using moist kitchen paper or a cotton bud.

Painting the large bowl

1 Using a medium paintbrush, paint the outer and inner rim of the bowl royal blue; leave to dry. Drying time will depend on the thickness of the paint, but it should be dry enough for you to continue painting in about 10 minutes; use a hair dryer to accelerate the process (see Painting Techniques, page 13).

2 Turn the bowl upside down on to a jam jar, then, using a decorator's paintbrush, drag the paintbrush down the outside surface of the bowl in long smooth strokes from top to bottom. Apply two further coats, allowing time to dry between each coat. Leave the bowl to dry for approximately 1 hour.

3 Turn the bowl the right way up, then using a fine paintbrush and working inside the bowl paint a 2.5cm (1in) wide stripe in deep yellow. Leave to dry, before painting a narrow royal blue stripe, below the yellow.

4 Paint three olives, dots and a sprig of foliage within each quarter using charcoal paint for the olives and leaf green for the foliage. For the leaves apply the paint with a medium paintbrush. Start the brush strokes near the stem and using a smooth continuous motion, flick the brush to produce a curved tail. Practise the brush stroke on a piece of paper first until you feel confident enough to apply the paint to the bowl. Use orange paint to apply a row of leaves to the edges of the yellow stripe.

Painting the small bowl

1 Turn the smaller bowl upside down on to a jam jar. Paint a 2.5cm (1in) stripe of deep yellow around the bowl; leave to dry. Using a fine paintbrush and leaf green, paint a fine line above the deep yellow; leave to dry. On the yellow stripe, paint two sprig stems within each quarter using leaf green paint. Add leaves using charcoal and orange paint on alternate stems. Add orange dots to the edge of the

yellow stripe, and charcoal dots between each stem. Leave the bowl to dry for 1 hour.

2 Turn the bowl the right way up, then using royal blue paint make a stripe around the inside rim of the bowl. Using leaf green, paint a row of small leaf shapes under the blue stripe.

Drying time

1 Allow the paint to air dry for a full 48 hours before hardening: if the paint has been applied thickly allow a longer drying time. Bubbling may occur during hardening if the paint is not completely dry.

Hardening the bowls

1 It is necessary to thermoharden water-based porcelain paint in a domestic oven to make it strong enough to stand up to normal use in the kitchen, although it would be advisable not to put the bowls in to the dishwasher. Place the bowls in a cold oven, and set the temperature to gas mark 2/3, 300/325°F (150/170°C). Bake for 30-35 minutes, timing from when the oven temperature stabilizes at the desired level. Turn the oven off when finished and leave to cool before removing the bowls from the oven.

Make tracings from these designs to transfer the outlines on to the bowls.

Animal Breakfast Set

Lavender and apricot have been used to give this chunky set of white china a fresh modern look. Stencil the complete dinner service using different farmyard animals; or you may prefer to paint just a set of mugs or egg cups. However much you paint, the china is sure to be much admired at meal-times

NOTE Read the paint instructions before using as some manufacturers do not recommend using the paint where it will come in contact with food or drink.

You will need
- White ceramic china
- Water-based porcelain paint – ultramarine blue, lavender, tangerine, light brown, orange, olive green, clay green
- Stencil film or acetate
- Felt-tipped pen, craft knife, cutting mat
- Stencil brush, fine paintbrush, small sponge
- Masking tape, scissors, self adhesive shapes
- Container of water, kitchen paper
- Alcohol, cloth, cotton bud

Preparing the china
1 Wash the china in warm soapy water and dry thoroughly.

2 Using kitchen paper, wipe the surface of the china with alcohol, then leave to dry: the alcohol will help the paint to adhere to the surface of the china.

Transferring the design
1 Lay stencil film or acetate over the animal motifs on page 61. Trace the designs carefully using a felt-tipped pen, leaving 2cm (1in) around each animal. Move the stencil as you cut, drawing the knife towards you.

2 Holding the stencil film or acetate on a cutting mat with one hand, cut out each animal shape using a sharp craft knife.

3 Attach the stencilled animals to the china using masking tape, bending them around the curves of the china.

Applying the paint
1 Lay the china on its side on a pad made from a tea-towel or kitchen paper. Apply a paint loaded stencil brush on to the area of china not covered by the stencil. Pounce the brush straight downwards on to the china, so that the paint does not get under the edges of the stencil.

2 Stencil the animals in the following colourways, using light and dark shades of apricot and lavender; apply the lighter shade before the darker, to give shading and detail to the animals. If you have difficulty in obtaining apricot coloured paint: mix tangerine and light brown together.

3 Paint the cow's body randomly in lavender, highlighted with ultramarine blue, then fill the remaining blank areas with apricot and orange; use lavender for the sheep's head and legs, and apricot for the body; for the pig, use lavender with apricot stripes across the body, shoulders and forelegs; use apricot and lavender for the chicken with ultramarine blue for the

tail feathers and head; for the goose and gosling paint the beak and feet in lavender, with apricot for the body, highlighted with orange; paint the rabbit's body using apricot with lavender patches and ears.

4 When the paint is dry, carefully remove the stencil and check for mistakes: spots of paint and smudges can easily be removed with a damp paintbrush.

Adding finishing touches

1 Use a stencil brush or sponge to add grass using two green shades; or add blades of grass using a fine brush. Finish the rims and edges of the china with a sponge.

the top. Allow the paint to dry before carefully removing the shapes, leaving a clean white star shape beneath.

Drying and hardening

1 Allow the paint to air dry for a full 48 hours before hardening. It is necessary to thermoharden water-based porcelain paint in a domestic oven to make it strong enough to stand up to normal use in the kitchen, although it would be advisable not to put it in the dishwasher. Place the china in a cold oven, and set the temperature to gas mark 2/3, 300/325°F (150/170°C). Bake for 30-35 minutes, timing from when the oven temperature stabilizes at the desired level. Turn the oven off and leave to cool.

2 Interesting border designs can be created using self-adhesive shapes like stars or spots (bought in packets from stationers): attach the shapes to the china, then sponge or stencil over

Use these animal shapes to create your own farmyard stencils.

Acknowledgements

Thanks to the designers for contributing such wonderful projects:
Floral Kitchen Set (page 14), Cheryl Owen
Painted Flower Pots (page 18), Caroline Palmer
Art Deco Cruet Set (page 24), Cheryl Owen
Maritime Tiles (page 28), Lynn Strange
Freehand Painted Mugs (page 34), Martin Penny
Finger Painted Teapots (page 38), Susan Penny
French Tiles (page 40), Julie Cook
Malachite Coffee Set (page 50), Cheryl Owen
Mediterranean Bowls (page 54), Cheryl Owen
Animal Breakfast Set (page 58), Caroline Palmer

Many thanks to Jon Stone for his inspirational photography;
Pebeo for supplying Porcelain 150 paint and outliner;
Lakeland Limited for supplying white china for the projects.

Other books in the Made Easy series

Mosaics (David & Charles, 1999)

Stamping (David & Charles, 1998)

Stencilling (David & Charles, 1998)

Glass Painting (David & Charles, 1998)

Silk Painting (David & Charles, 1998)

Suppliers

ColArt Fine Art & Graphics Ltd
Whitefriars Avenue
Harrow
Middlesex HA3 5RH
Tel: 0181 427 4343
Mail order service
(Lefranc & Bourgeois cold set ceramique paint)

Craft World (Head office only)
No 8 North Street,
Guildford
Surrey GU1 4AF
Tel: 07000 757070
Retail shops nationwide, telephone for local
store
(Craft warehouse)

Debenhams PLC (Customer services)
1 Welbeck Street
London W1 1DF
Retail shops nationwide, telephone for local
store
Tel: 0171 408 4444
(White china)

Hobby Crafts (Head office only)
River Court
Southern Sector
Bournemouth International Airport
Christchurch
Dorset BH23 6SE
Tel: 0800 272387 freephone
Retail shops nationwide, telephone for local
store
(Craft warehouse)

Home Crafts Direct
PO Box 38
Leicester LE1 9BU
Tel: 0116 251 3139
Mail order service
(Craft equipment)

Lakeland Ltd
Alexandra Buildings
Windermere
Cumbria LA23 1BQ
Tel: 01539 488100
Retail shops nationwide and mail order service
(White china)

Marks & Spencer PLC (Customer services)
Michael House
Baker Street
London
W1A 4DN
Tel: 0171 935 4422
Retail shops nationwide, telephone for local
store
(White china)

Pebeo Paints (Distributor - office address only)
Philip and Tacey Ltd
North Way
Andover
Hampshire
SP10 5BA
Tel: 01264 332171
Telephone for your local retail stockist
(Pebeo water-based porcelain paint, outliner
paste, brushes)

Index

Page numbers in italics refer to main photograph

Acknowledgements, 62
Alcohol, cleaning with 13
Animal Breakfast Set, 58–61, *59*
Art Deco Cruet Set, 24–27, *25*

Bagging 11
Bowls, 54, 58
Brushes, types of 6, 9, cleaning 12
Butter dish, 14

Carbon paper, 8
Ceramic paint, types of 7
China, choosing 6
Cleaning, brushes 12,
Cruet set, 24
Cups and saucers, 50

Decorative effects, 7
Dragging, 11
Drying, 13

Egg cup, 58
Essential equipment, 6

Finger Painted Teapots, 38–39, *39*
Finger painting 11, 38
Floral flowerpot, 21
Floral Kitchen Set, 14–17, *15*
Flower pots, 18
Freehand Painted Mugs, 34–37, *35*
Freehand, 11
French Tiles, 40–49, *41*
Fruit flowerpot, 18

Gloss medium 7, 9, 28

Hardening, 7, 13
Hints and Tips, 13

Introduction to Ceramic Painting, 6–7

Jug, 16, 58

Lines, freehand 11, outline 10

Malachite Coffee Set, 50–53, *51*
Malachite effect, 12, 53
Maritime Tiles, 28–33, *29*
Masking tape grids, 8, 21
Matt medium 7, 10, 22
Mediterranean Bowls, 54–57, *55*
Mistakes, correcting 13
Mosaic flowerpot, 21
Mugs, 34, 58

Oven temperature, 7
Outliner, 7, 10, 14

Paint, applying 9, mixing 9
Painted Flower Pots, 18–23, *19*
Painting Techniques, 9–12
Paper masks, 8, 60
Plates, 50
Porcelain paint, 7

Scratching, 10
Speed drying, 13
Sponging, 11
Stencils, using 8, 31, 58
Suppliers, 63

Teapots, 38
Tiles, 28, 40
Towelling, 11, 38
Transferring the design, 8
Tray, 24

Undercoat, filler 12, 18
Utensil pot, 14

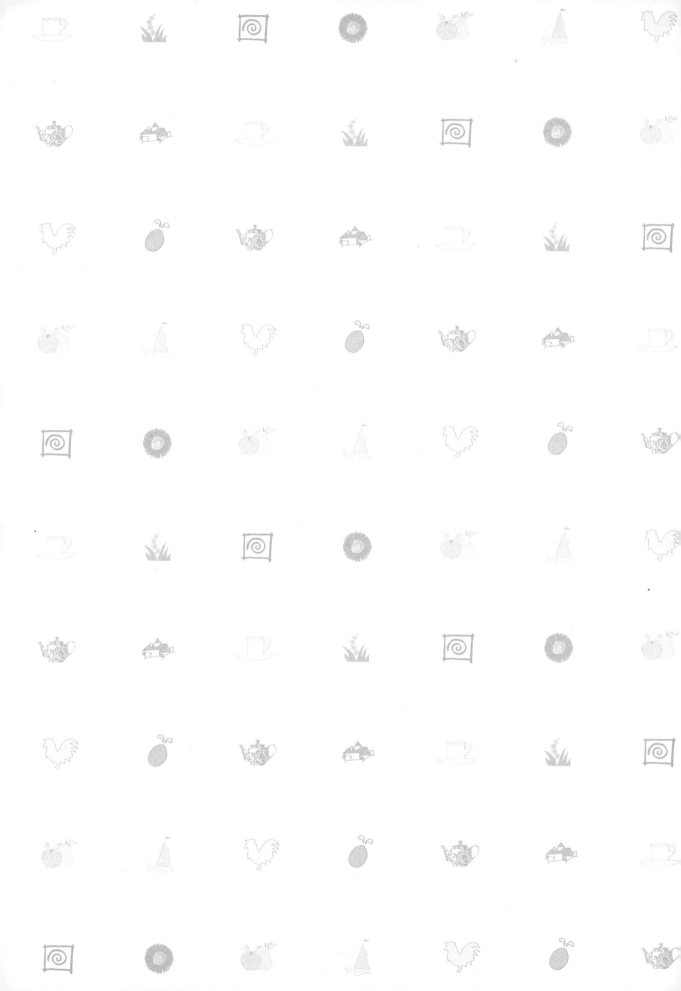